THE
HEALING POWER
OF OLIVE OIL

Gayle Alleman, M.S., R.D.

Publications International, Ltd.

CHAPTER ONE
OLIVE OIL'S HEALING SECRETS

Olive oil works to keep hearts healthy, may reduce inflam-mation and the risk of certain cancers, and might even play a role in controlling diabetes and weight. Clearly, there is more to it than great taste!

A diet that is rich in olive oil has enhanced the health of people living in the Mediterranean region for thousands of years. Within the past century, however, olive oil's benefits have been scientifically investigated, acknowledged, and proclaimed across the globe.

Many theories exist as to where olive trees originated, but one that is fairly well accepted is that they first grew in Asia Minor, the land bridge between Europe and Asia that is now home to Turkey and Syria. Evidence shows that humans in this area were using olives more than 8,000 years ago.

Historians believe olive use spread throughout the rest of the Mediterranean region about 6,000 years ago. Phoeni-cians carried olive trees to what is now southern Europe, as well as to Egypt and other areas along the North African coast. Olive remnants have been found inside Egyptian tombs, signifying the important role they played in that culture.

Later, the Greeks and Romans put olives to good use. People in both of these ancient civilizations used olive oil to counter-

THE HARDY OLIVE TREE

An olive tree can live 1,000 years or more. Even if the tree dies or is cut or damaged, sprouts from its roots can grow into full-size, fruit-bearing trees. Olive trees succeed in climates in which there are mildly cold winters (they need cooler temperatures to set the buds that later form the fruit) and long, hot summers. During the growing season, olives need a lot of dry heat. The tough trees don't need much water and can tolerate temperatures as low as 10 degrees Fahrenheit for brief periods of time.

act poisons and to treat open wounds, insect bites, headaches, and stomach and digestive problems. They also applied olive oil to the body before bathing (it functioned as soap) and then again afterward to moisturize the skin and to form a barrier against dirt and the sun's rays. The Romans took olives along in their travels, planting them wherever they went and spreading their beneficial qualities to many regions.

HEALING THROUGH THE AGES

The olive's medicinal properties have helped people for thousands of years, and those who reaped the benefits of the fruit didn't keep its wonderful secrets to themselves. During the past several hundred years, olive trees made their way around the world to areas in which they could be successfully cultivated, including North America, South America, New Zealand, Australia, and Japan.

As the olive migrated, folk remedies using olive oil evolved to reflect the times and maladies of different regions. Olive oil was taken by mouth, spread on the skin, and dropped into the ears or nose. People considered it both a cure and a preventative measure for many afflictions. Here are some popular folk remedies that have been used over the years:

- Take a spoonful or two to treat an upset stomach, difficult digestion, constipation, or to reduce the body's absorption of alcohol from alcoholic beverages.
- Apply to skin to prevent dryness and wrinkles, to soften the skin, and to treat acne.
- Use on the hair to make it shiny and to treat dandruff.
- Strengthen nails by soaking them in warm olive oil.
- Ease aching muscles by massaging them with olive oil.
- Lower blood pressure by boiling olive tree leaves and drinking the "tea."
- Clear nasal congestion with drops of olive oil in the nose.

A word of caution: Using olive oil as a folk remedy may not be safe for children. In November 2005, an article in *Archives of Pediatrics & Adolescent Medicine* and an ensuing report by Reuters Health cautioned caregivers against giving infants and young children a dose of olive oil to treat digestive problems, fussiness, and stuffy noses. Oil administered through the mouth or nose may be inhaled into the lungs and can cause lipoid pneumonia. You should always consult a pediatrician before trying any treatment on a child.

Chronic diseases and conditions that are caused, in part, by unhealthy foods and sedentary lifestyles plague many societies today, especially those in the Western world. The good news is olive oil may help with the worst of them, including heart disease, hypertension (high blood pressure), metabolic syndrome, inflammation, cancer, diabetes, and problems associated with obesity.

A GOD'S GIFT

According to Greek mythology, Athena, daughter of Zeus, invented the olive tree and gave it to the people of Athens as a gift. As the story goes, Athena planted the first olive tree on a hill now known as the Acropolis. Some say the olive tree that grows there today comes from the roots of that original tree. The Greeks appreciated the olive so much that they named their capital city after the goddess who gave them the tree.

These conditions take many years to develop, but inactivity and consumption of too much solid fat (saturated fat and *trans* fat) greatly increase your chances of having to deal with them. However, olive oil and diets rich in monounsaturated fat may help combat the development of some chronic conditions.

FAT FACTS

It may seem remarkable that such a small dietary change—switching from one type of fat to another—can significantly impact your health, but as you will see here, the type of fat you fancy really matters. Some fats, especially those in olive oil, have more healthful properties than others, so to make the right choices, it's important to know the differences among the various kinds.

There are four types of dietary fats, also known as fatty acids, and each has different health effects, depending on its source and how it is produced.

Monounsaturated fat. This is the healthiest type of fat. It promotes heart health and might help prevent cancer and a host of other ailments. Monounsaturated fat helps lower "bad" low-density lipoprotein (LDL) cholesterol levels without negatively affecting the "good" high-density lipoprotein (HDL) cholesterol. Olive oil, peanut oil, canola oil, and avocados are rich in healthy monounsaturated fat.

Polyunsaturated fat. Polyunsaturated fat is moderately healthy. It lowers LDL cholesterol, which is good, but it also reduces levels of artery-clearing HDL cholesterol. Polyunsaturated fat is usually liquid at room temperature and is the predominant type of fatty acid in soybean oil, safflower oil, corn oil, and several other vegetable oils.

Saturated fat. This fat is unhealthy because the body turns it into artery-clogging cholesterol, which is harmful to your heart. Saturated fat is mostly found in animal products and is solid at room temperature. It is the white fat you see along the edge or marbled throughout a piece of meat and is the fat in the skin of poultry. It is also "hidden" in whole milk and foods made from whole milk, as well as in tropical oils such as coconut oil. Dietitians recommend that people eat only small amounts of saturated fat.

Trans *fat.* *Trans* fat is the worst type of fat; you're best off avoiding it. Most *trans* fat is manufactured by forcing hydrogen into liquid polyunsaturated fat in a process called hydrogenation. The process can create a solid fat product— margarine is made this way. Hydrogenation gives foods a longer shelf life and helps stabilize their flavors, but your body pays a big price.

The body recognizes *trans* fat as being saturated and converts it to cholesterol, which raises LDL levels and lowers HDL levels. What's worse is that, unlike saturated fat, *trans* fat disrupts cell membranes. Cell membranes are comprised of uniformly configured fatty acid chains that are linked together through tight chemical bonds. When *trans* fat works its way into the chains, it alters these bonds and creates "leaks" in the cell membrane. This action upsets the flow of nutrients and waste products into and out of the cell and may be linked to reduced immune function and possibly cancer.

Fried foods in restaurants may contain large amounts of *trans* fats if they are cooked in partially hydrogenated oil. However, thanks to pressure from consumer and health groups, some restaurants are now using liquid soybean oil rather than partially hydrogenated soybean oil. This costs the restaurant a little more but is healthier for you.

Many fast-food restaurant chains display a nutrition facts brochure—check this literature to see how much *trans* fat is in each food. When dining elsewhere, ask your server whether the cooks use a *trans*-fat-free oil. When frying foods at home, be sure to use a liquid oil, such as heart-healthy olive oil, rather than shortening, which is created by hydrogenation.

Meat and milk are also sources of *trans* fat, but they contain very little. These naturally occurring *trans* fats do not appear to have any negative health consequences.

MAJORITY RULES

The fat we eat is made up of varying amounts of the different fats just described. When a food is predominantly comprised of one type of fat, we call it by that name. For instance, as the chart on page 9 shows, olive oil is high in monounsaturated fat. Even though it contains other types of fat, olive oil is referred to as a monounsaturated fat. You'll see at a glance that olive oil outweighs any other fat when it comes to health-promoting monounsaturated fat content.

An Olive's Omegas

There are two important polyunsaturated fats that are essential for human health, but the body cannot make them. This means we must get them from the foods we eat. These two essential fatty acids are alpha-linolenic acid, an omega-3 fatty acid, and linoleic acid, an omega-6 fatty acid. The body gets both from olive oil.

Omega-3 oils are the healthiest. They are part of a group of substances called prostaglandins that help keep blood cells from sticking together, increase blood flow, and reduce inflammation. This makes omega-3 oils useful in preventing cardiovascular disease as well as inflammatory conditions, such as arthritis.

Omega-6 oils are healthy, too, but they are not quite as helpful as omega-3's. Omega-6's can help form prostaglandins that are similarly beneficial to the ones produced by omega-3's, but they can also produce harmful prostaglandins. The

Your Right to Know

By rule of the United States Food and Drug Administration (FDA), as of January 1, 2006, food manufacturers are required to list the amount of *trans* fat on nutrition labels. The FDA rule states that the amount of *trans* fat in a serving should be listed by weight (in grams) on a separate line under saturated fat.

However, according to the FDA, food manufacturers are allowed to list the amount of *trans* fat per serving in a food as zero grams if the actual amount is less than 0.5 gram. That is why you may see a product that has partially hydrogenated vegetable oil listed as an ingredient but has *trans* fat content listed as zero grams.

Type of fat	% monounsat- urated fat	% poly- unsaturated fat	% saturated fat	% other elements
Olive oil	74	8	14	4
Canola oil	59	30	7	4
Peanut oil	46	32	17	5
Corn oil	24	59	13	4
Soybean oil	23	58	14	4
Sunflower oil	20	65	10	5
Safflower oil	14	75	6	5
Walnut oil	23	63	9	5
Palm kernel oil	11	2	81	6
Palm oil	37	9	50	4
Coconut oil	6	2	86	6
Butter	30	4	62	4
Shortening	30	37	29	4
*Tallow	42	4	50	4

*Rendered fat of cattle or sheep

Note: Due to rounding, not all values will equal 100 percent for each type of fat

Source: U.S. Department of Agriculture, Agricultural Research Service. 2005. USDA National Nutrient Database for Standard Reference, Release 18. Nutrient Data Laboratory Home Page, www.ars.usda.gov/ba/bhnrc/ndl

unfavorable prostaglandins increase blood-cell stickiness and promote cardiovascular disease, and they also appear to be linked to the formation of cancer. To encourage your body to make beneficial prostaglandins from omega-6 oils, you should decrease the amount of animal fat you eat. Too much animal fat tends to push your body into using omega-6 oils to make the unfavorable prostaglandins rather than the helpful ones.

The research is inconclusive about how much omega-6 you should eat compared to the amount of omega-3. Many researchers suggest consuming one to four times more omega-6's than omega-3's, but the typical American eats anywhere from 11 to 30 times more omega-6's than omega-3's.

The U.S. Dietary Reference Intakes for essential fatty acids recommends the consumption of omega-6 and omega-3 fats in a ratio of 10-to-1. This means consuming ten times more omega-6's than omega-3's. Lucky for us, nature provided that exact ratio of fat in each little olive. The linoleic-to-linolenic ratio is about 10-to-1.

GET HEART HELP FROM OLIVE OIL

Research abounds regarding the benefits of monounsaturated fat. Other studies are showing that the potent phytochemicals (those substances in plants that may have health benefits for people) in olive oil—specifically, a group called phenolic compounds—appear to promote good health.

Studies have shown that a phytochemical in olive oil called hydroxytyrosol "thins" the blood. Other phytochemicals reduce inflammation of the blood vessels, prevent oxidation of fats in the bloodstream, protect blood vessel walls, and dilate the blood vessels for improved circulation.

CHOLESTEROL COMBATANT

Olive oil boosts heart health by keeping a lid on cholesterol levels. It lowers total cholesterol, LDL cholesterol, and triglyceride levels. Some studies show that it does not affect HDL cholesterol; others show that it slightly increases HDL levels.

A 2002 article in *The American Journal of Medicine* reported that total cholesterol levels decrease an average of 13.4 percent and LDL cholesterol levels drop an average of 18 percent when people replace saturated fat with monounsaturated fat in their diets. These results seem to hold for middle-age and older adults who have high blood cholesterol levels.

The polyphenolic compounds (types of phytochemicals) in olive oil appear to play a big part in protecting blood vessels. Three polyphenols, oleuropein, tyrosol, and hydroxytyrosol, are believed to be particularly helpful. Numerous studies have shown that polyphenols and monounsaturated fat help keep LDL cholesterol from being oxidized and sticking to the inner walls of arteries, forming the plaque that hampers blood flow. When plaque forms in arteries, the risk of heart disease or stroke increases.

Polyphenolic compounds are also responsible for preserving and protecting two enzymes—glutathione reductase and glutathione peroxidase—that fight free radicals in the body. Without enzymes like these, free radicals can damage healthy cells, potentially leading to the development of cancer and other serious health problems.

Research reported in the November 2005 issue of the *Journal of the American College of Cardiology* provides

JUICE VS. SEEDS

Olives are a fruit, and when you press them, you get juice. This juice is rich not only in oil but also in potent phytochemicals and several vitamins. Need another reason to choose olive oil? It's a more natural product than seed oils.

Seeds, such as sunflower, soybean, or rapeseed (the source of canola oil), undergo much more processing to extract their oil. They are not merely crushed or pressed to remove their oil; they are typically processed with heat and sometimes chemicals to gain access to their tiny oil reserves. Even "cold-pressed" seed oils require heat of up to 120 degrees Fahrenheit. Therefore, seed oil is more highly processed than what we get from simple olive juice.

compelling evidence for the advantages of olive oil's polyphenolic compounds. In the study, 21 otherwise-healthy Spanish volunteers who had high blood cholesterol levels were given 2.5 tablespoons of either virgin olive oil that was rich in phenolic compounds or olive oil that had much less of these phytonutrients as part of their breakfast. Careful measurements for the next four hours showed that those who consumed the phenolic-rich olive oil experienced:

♦ An increase in the dilation of the interior walls of blood vessels. The more dilated a vessel is, the freer the circulation and the less work the heart has to do to pump blood through the body.

♦ An increase in the amount of nitric oxide in the bloodstream. Nitric oxide is a strong vasodilator (an agent that causes the blood vessels to dilate, or expand). Nitric oxide relaxes the smooth muscles that line artery walls, thus improving circulation. It also inhibits the clumping of blood cells called platelets, reducing the risk of blood clots. Oleuropein is the phytonutrient in olive oil that is responsible for stimulating the production of nitric oxide.

Results such as these suggest that adding a small amount of phenolic-rich olive oil to the diet (or, better yet, substituting olive oil for harmful saturated fats in the diet) can make a significant impact on reducing atherosclerosis and the cascade of events that leads to heart disease. The researchers identified this finding as especially important because, in other studies, meals high in saturated fat, such as hamburg-

NOW READ THIS!

The FDA approved a health claim statement in November 2004 for optional use on labels of foods that are rich in monounsaturated fat and low in cholesterol and saturated fat. It reads:

"Limited and not conclusive scientific evidence suggests that eating about 2 tablespoons (23 grams) of olive oil daily may reduce the risk of coronary heart disease due to the monounsaturated fat in olive oil. To achieve this possible benefit, olive oil is to replace a similar amount of saturated fat and not increase the total number of calories you eat in a day. One serving of this product contains [x] grams of olive oil."

The last sentence is optional when the claim is used on actual olive oil labels.

ers and french fries, have been shown to create the opposite effect. Such meals inhibit the normal and healthy function of blood vessels and constrict blood flow.

Looking at the two sets of results together, then, further enhances support for the cardiac benefits of using olive oil in place of saturated and *trans* fats in the diet.

THE MEDITERRANEAN DIET

The Mediterranean diet (one that is high in monounsaturated fat from olive oil and moderate in calories) made headlines when an Italian study appeared in the *Journal of the American Medical Association* in September 2004. The study followed two groups of 90 people who had metabolic syndrome (see "What Is Metabolic Syndrome?" on the next page) for two years. During the study, both groups increased their activity levels by 60 percent.

One study group was given detailed instructions about how to increase the whole grains, vegetables, fruits, nuts, and olive oil in their diets. The other 90 subjects consumed a "control" diet (50 percent to 60 percent of calories from carbohydrates, 15 percent to 20 percent of calories from protein, and less than 30 percent of calories from fat). After two years, those on the Mediterranean diet showed improvement in cholesterol levels, significantly less C-reactive protein in their blood, less insulin resistance, more weight loss, and improvements in the condition of their blood-vessel walls.

A follow-up study two years later revealed only 40 of the original 90 people on the Mediterranean diet still had metabolic syndrome, compared with 78 people in the control group.

WHAT IS METABOLIC SYNDROME?

Metabolic syndrome is a cluster of conditions that increases the risk of coronary artery disease and type 2 diabetes. In general, if a person has three or more of the conditions listed below, he or she likely has metabolic syndrome (which is sometimes called insulin-resistance syndrome).

- Excess weight, especially in the abdominal area
- High LDL cholesterol, low HDL cholesterol, and high triglyceride levels
- High blood pressure
- Insulin resistance (the body doesn't respond to insulin appropriately)
- "Thick" blood that is prone to clumping and clotting (as indicated by high levels of a substance called plasminogen activator inhibitor-1 in the blood)
- Inflamed blood vessels (as indicated by high levels in the blood of a compound named C-reactive protein)

MORE HEARTFELT EVIDENCE

A French study published in the *International Journal of Obesity-Related Metabolic Disorders* in June 2003 added to the evidence in favor of olive oil as a heart helper. Thirty-two people ate either a high-carbohydrate diet or one that was high in monounsaturated fat. After eight weeks, the people who consumed lots of monounsaturated fats had better triglyceride levels than those participants who were on the diet high in carbohydrates. Those who ate more monounsaturated fat also had less oxidative stress, a condition in which there are more free radicals than the body can handle and/or low levels of antioxidants. This condition puts the arteries at risk of damage and encourages heart disease.

The diet rich in monounsaturated fat also appeared to protect against smooth-muscle-cell proliferation, another risk factor for atherosclerosis.

OLIVE OIL—A BOON TO BLOOD PRESSURE

An Italian study published in the December 2003 issue of the *Journal of Hypertension* reviewed numerous research projects that looked at various factors that affect blood pressure. The review indicated that unsaturated fat reduced blood pressure. The researchers went on to say that olive oil in particular was uniquely able to reduce high blood pressure—much more than sunflower oil.

A large study that appeared a year later in *The American Journal of Clinical Nutrition* looked at the diets of more than 20,000 Greeks who did not have high blood pressure when the study began. The study found that those who ate the typical Mediterranean diet had lower blood pressure. Further, when the effects of olive oil consumption were compared to those of vegetable oil consumption, olive oil was shown to have a more positive impact on blood pressure.

Spain is another country where olive oil is a staple in many households. People there typically use olive oil, sunflower oil (a mostly polyunsaturated oil), or a mixture of the two. Researchers in one Spanish study wanted to learn the role each of these oils played in blood pressure, as well as how the oils held up to cultural cooking methods in which oil is heated to a high temperature for frying and later reused several times.

The study, which was published in the December 2003 issue of *The American Journal of Clinical Nutrition*, examined samples of cooking oil from the kitchens of 538 study participants. Researchers measured the blood pressure and conducted blood tests on those participants and nearly 500 more "control" subjects. Here's what they found:

- Olive oil was resistant to heat degradation.

- Mixed oil and sunflower oil degraded more than olive oil alone when heated and reused.

- Those who used sunflower oil, whether or not it had deteriorated, had higher blood pressure levels than those who used olive oil.

- The higher the monounsaturated fat consumption, the lower the blood pressure tended to be.

At the end of the study, the researchers concluded that because olive oil does a better job of maintaining its healthful properties and because it positively influences blood cholesterol and blood pressure levels, it should be the oil of choice in everyone's kitchen.

COOLING INFLAMMATION

Inflammation within the body may occur in response to cigarette smoking or eating large amounts of saturated fat and *trans* fat. In overweight or obese people, excess fat from fat cells can float through the bloodstream and cause inflammation. Although inflammation can help the body, it can also hurt.

Certain dietary fats cause more of an inflammatory response than others. *Trans* fat and the saturated fat in animal foods stimulate inflammation. To a smaller extent, polyunsaturated fat in foods such as safflower oil, sunflower oil, and corn oil triggers inflammation, as well. Again, this is where olive oil helps. Olive oil's phytonutrients—in this case phenolic compounds called squalene, beta-sitosterol, and tyrosol—don't cause inflammation: they reduce it.

WHAT IS INFLAMMATION?

Inflammation is the immune system's first line of defense against injury and infection. When an injury occurs, such as a simple cut on the finger, a set of events takes place within your body that forms a blood clot, fights infection, and begins the healing process. Inflammation is painful because blood vessels dilate upstream of the injury to bring more blood and nutrients to the injured area, but they constrict at the injury site. These actions result in fluids from the bloodstream pooling in tissue around the injury, which causes swelling and pressure that stimulate nerves and cause pain.

In some individuals, the immune system gets confused and begins to view some of the body's own healthy cells as "foreign invaders." It therefore directs an immune response—complete with inflammation—at healthy tissues, harming or even destroying them. This misdirected attack results in what's called an autoimmune disorder ("auto" meaning self). Rheumatoid arthritis and certain types of thyroid disease are autoimmune disorders. Asthma, too, is the result of inflammation gone awry.

When inflammation continues unabated for long periods of time, damage can occur in organs, such as the colon, or in blood vessels. Indeed, chronic inflammation within the body is looking more and more like a serious contributor to cardiovascular (heart and blood vessel) disease. Inflammation may damage the inner lining of blood vessels, which encourages plaque deposits to form. Inflammation may also cause plaque in arteries to break off and travel downstream, where it can become lodged and stop blood flow to a crucial artery that provides oxygen to important body parts, such as your heart or brain. When this happens, a heart attack or stroke (respectively) can occur.

Chronic inflammation within the body can wreak havoc on other body parts besides arteries. A team led by researchers at the Johns Hopkins Medical Institutions found that chronic inflammation of the colon might increase the risk of colon cancer. A ten-year study of more than 20,000 patients suggested a link between chronic inflammation and this disease, although a direct cause-and-effect relationship has not yet been established. These preliminary findings were discussed in the February 2004 edition of the *Journal of the American Medical Association*.

Yet another condition that appears to be linked to inflammation is type 2 diabetes, the most common form of diabetes that affects an estimated 20 million Americans. Having excess body fat seems to increase inflammation. As inflammation increases, so does insulin resistance. As insulin resistance increases, blood glucose levels rise and the risk of type 2 diabetes skyrockets.

Scientists have discovered that inflammation can be reduced with low daily doses of aspirin or other nonsteroidal anti-inflammatory drugs (NSAIDs), which in turn appear to reduce the risk of diseases caused by inflammation. Fortunately, not only does olive oil not prompt the kind of inflammation other types of fat can, it actually has some ability to *reduce* inflammation, thanks to those helpful phytochemicals (squalene, beta-sitosterol, and tyrosol). So consuming olive oil on a regular basis may help decrease the risk of conditions linked to inflammation.

WHAT IS OLEOCANTHAL AND HOW CAN IT HELP YOU?

An article published by Philadelphia researchers in the September 2005 issue of *Nature* identified a compound in olive oil called oleocanthal that has anti-inflammatory action. Their studies revealed that this compound can act like ibuprofen and other anti-inflammatory medications.

Olive oils differ widely in the amount of oleocanthal they possess. To get an idea of how oleocanthal-rich your olive oil of choice is, researchers suggest taking a sip of the oil to "see how strongly it stings the back of the throat." The stronger the sting, the more oleocanthal the oil contains. Fifty grams (nearly a quarter of a cup of olive oil) provides the same amount of anti-inflammatory action as 10 percent of the standard adult dose of ibuprofen.

Obviously, eating enough olive oil to equal a whole dose of ibuprofen is not a practical way to decrease your inflammation and pain. But consuming a moderate amount of olive oil daily—in place of most of the other fat you typically consume—over the long term may lessen chronic inflammation throughout the body and bloodstream. It might even somewhat diminish asthma and rheumatoid arthritis symptoms.

OLIVE OIL'S POSSIBLE ROLE IN CANCER PREVENTION

Many medical researchers believe cancers of the colon, prostate, and breast are linked to dietary fat intake. Typically, high-fat diets were blamed, but research is beginning to suggest the more important factor may be the type of fat in the diet. In Spain, Italy, and Greece, where olive oil is used in most households, cancer incidence is much lower than in northern Europe and the United States, where olive oil use isn't as widespread.

There is plenty of controversy regarding whether olive oil can play any part in helping to prevent breast cancer, but women who follow a Mediterranean-style diet appear to have a lower risk of the disease. A study published in the March 2005 issue of the *Annals of Oncology* showed that oleic acid, the principal monounsaturated fat in olive oil, dramatically decreased the growth of aggressive forms of breast tumors in test tubes. When oleic acid was combined with the commonly used breast cancer drug Herceptin, the effectiveness of the drug was vastly improved.

A review of studies conducted between 1990 and 2003 that was presented in the July 2005 issue of the *World Journal of Surgical Oncology* noted a direct association between saturated fat intake and breast cancer incidence. The more saturated fat consumed, the higher the incidence of breast cancer. In addition, the researchers reported an inverse relationship between the disease and oleic acid: The more oleic acid a woman ate, the lower her risk of breast cancer.

On the other hand, a different meta-analysis, published in the September 2004 *International Journal of Cancer*, analyzed ten studies that involved more than 2,000 cases of breast cancer. It found opposite results—the more oleic acid consumed, the higher the rate of breast cancer.

Clearly, more studies are needed to determine olive oil's real relationship to breast cancer. In the meantime, moderation may be the key to reaping the benefits of olive oil without increasing risk.

DIABETES AND OLIVE OIL

People living with diabetes have to work hard to keep their blood sugar, also called blood glucose, levels under control. One way to do so is to eat a diet that is fairly low in carbohydrates. Because people with diabetes are also at an elevated risk of developing heart disease, they are advised to limit their intake of dietary fat.

Lately, researchers and nutritionists have been debating the best type of eating pattern for people with diabetes. Some research indicates that a diet high in monounsaturated fat may be better than a low-fat, low-carbohydrate diet.

Numerous studies have suggested that people with diabetes who consume a diet high in monounsaturated fat have the same level of control over blood sugar levels as those who eat a low-fat diabetic diet. But monounsaturated fat also helps keep triglyceride levels in check, reduce LDL cholesterol levels, and increase HDL cholesterol levels.

Researchers in Spain published an article in *The American Journal of Clinical Nutrition* in September 2003 that concluded calorie-controlled diabetic diets high in monounsaturated fat do not cause weight gain and are more pleasing to eat than low-fat diets. The researchers determined that a diet high in monounsaturated fat is a good idea for people with diabetes.

Research is still inconsistent as to whether monounsaturated fat actually plays a role in stabilizing blood glucose levels, but evidence is leaning in that direction. A review of a number of studies, which was done by German researchers and appeared in the official journal of the German Diabetes Association, found that blood glucose levels were lower in people who ate a diet rich in monounsaturated fat than in people who ate a low-fat diet. Further, they said increasing monounsaturated-fat intake lowered LDL cholesterol levels in some, though not all, subjects.

WEIGHTY ISSUES

Medical professionals are greatly concerned about the obesity problem in the United States. Obesity often comes hand-in-hand with high levels of cholesterol and lipids in the blood (hyperlipidemia), heart disease, high blood pressure, diabetes, certain cancers, and a higher rate of premature death.

Health-care professionals often recommend following a very low-fat diet in order to lose weight. But there may be some good news for those overweight folks who struggle to limit dietary fat. Research suggests that replacing other types of fats with monounsaturated fat, especially olive oil, helps people lose a moderate amount of weight without additional food restriction or physical activity. So just imagine what adding a lower-calorie diet and increased physical activity (which are always good ideas) to the consumption of monounsaturated fats like olive oil could do for your weight-loss efforts.

FDA scientists reviewed many different studies when they evaluated whether to allow health claims for monounsaturated fat on food labels in 2003. The researchers wanted to ensure that a proposed recommendation to eat 13.5 grams (one tablespoon) of olive oil per day wouldn't contribute to weight gain in the American population. A number of studies showed that when people substituted monounsaturated-fat-rich olive oil for saturated fat, they either maintained their weight or lost weight. A diet high in monounsaturated fat and low in carbohydrates resulted in more weight loss than a low-fat, high-carbohydrate diet.

MARVELOUS POLYPHENOLS

Polyphenols are advantageous not only to human health but also to the health of the olive. Phenolic compounds protect the olive, prevent oxidation of its oil, and allow it to stay in good condition longer. In addition, they increase the shelf life of olive oil and contribute to its tart flavor.

What's more, the FDA determined that eating 13.5 grams of monounsaturated fat in a dietary pattern low in saturated fat and cholesterol would reduce total blood cholesterol and LDL cholesterol levels by an average of 5 percent, resulting in a 10 percent decrease in coronary heart disease. However, the FDA did not approve this particular claim for food labels. Instead, the agency approved a stronger claim linking the consumption of 23 grams (about two tablespoons) of olive oil to a decreased risk of coronary heart disease. (See the "Now Read This!" sidebar on page 13 to read this claim.)

Another study showed that when people ate monounsaturated fat, they ate less. For example, when served bread with olive oil, participants ate 23 percent less bread than when they ate it with butter, a saturated fat. Scientists speculate that because monounsaturated fat is more satisfying than other types of fat, people eat less of it. Additionally, the body's metabolism of monounsaturated fat after a meal appears to be different from the metabolism of saturated fat. This difference in metabolism may be what causes slight weight loss. (Researchers haven't yet determined exactly how this works.)

Several other studies indicate that monounsaturated fat may even enhance the body's ability to break down stored fat. A study of rats that was published in the *British Journal of Nutrition* in December 2003 found that monounsaturated fat facilitated the release of fat from rats' fat cells. Also, insulin became less able to prevent the breakdown of fat, which made it easier for fat cells to release their stored fat for elimination by the body. Results were opposite in the rats that were given polyunsaturated fat. Thus, an increase in monounsaturated fat in the diet (along with, presumably, an equivalent decrease in saturated-fat intake) may help with weight loss.

A pair of studies published in the *Asia-Pacific Journal of Clinical Nutrition* in 2004 looked at whether a diet high in monounsaturated fat was more effective for weight loss than a diet that was low in total fat. The studies also examined the effects of a Mediterranean diet on blood cholesterol and triglyceride levels.

The two studies tracked a total of 255 participants (155 in one study, 100 in the other) for 15 months. Researchers concluded that a Mediterranean diet was very effective for weight loss in the short term (3 months) *and* 15 months later. Participants who completed the study's initial three-month program had better weight-loss results and regained less weight after 15 months than those who did not complete the program. These results were comparable to or even better than the typical results found in studies of common weight-loss programs and combination diet/drug therapy.

The study also found that a Mediterranean diet had favorable effects on HDL cholesterol and triglyceride levels at three months and a neutral effect on total cholesterol and LDL cholesterol levels. (A neutral effect means there were no significant changes in these measurements.) In the study with 155 patients, HDL levels increased by 9.6 percent and triglyceride levels decreased by 31.6 percent.

OH, THOSE POWERFUL OLIVES

Not all olives are created equal. Just as some varieties of apples are sweeter or more tart than others, different varieties of olives yield varying amounts of oil. Large black olives typically purchased in a can from the grocer's shelf may contain as little as 7 percent oil. These are table olives. At the other end of the spectrum, some olives contain up to 35 percent oil. These are the ones used for pressing.

No matter where the oil comes from, increasing the amount of olive oil in your diet is a great way to eat your way to good health. Find out how to replace your bad fats with olive oil in the next chapter.

Nutrient Content of Olive Oil

Nutrient	Amount in one tablespoon	Daily amount recommended for the average adult (if applicable)
Calories	119	2,000
Protein	0 g	46 g (women) 56 g (men)
Carbohydrates	0 g	130 g
Fiber	0 g	25 g (women) 38 g (men)
Total fat	13.5 g	65 g maximum
Monounsaturated fat	9.85 g	Not applicable
Polyunsaturated fat	1.421 g	Not applicable
Saturated fat	1.864 g	20 g
Cholesterol	0 g	300 mg
Phytosterol	30 g	2 g
Vitamin E	1.94 mg	2 g
Vitamin K	8.1 mcg	90 mcg (women) 120 mcg (men)
Iron	0.08 mg	18 mg (women) 8 mg (men)

g = grams, mg = milligrams, mcg = micrograms

Note: Olive oil is not a source of any vitamins other than vitamins E and K and is not a source of any mineral other than iron.

Source: U.S. Department of Agriculture, Agricultural Research Service. 2005. USDA National Nutrient Database for Standard Reference, Release 18. Nutrient Data Laboratory Home Page, www.ars.usda.gov/ba/bhnrc/ndl

CHAPTER TWO
THE MANY FACES OF OLIVE OIL

A visit to the local market for olive oil may make your head spin. With dozens of choices, which one is best? Which has the most healing properties? Which is best right out of the bottle, and which is best for cooking? Fear not, because your olive oil IQ is about to increase.

Once you choose the olive oil that is right for you and your recipes, you must be careful using and storing it to preserve its healthful qualities. You'll be well rewarded for your careful selection and storage when you experience olive oil's aroma and flavor in your favorite dishes.

FROM TREE TO TABLE

The craft of turning olives into oil has been honed in the Mediterranean region over thousands of years, and techniques have been passed down from generation to generation. The process is truly a regional art. The method used in Greece is different from the one used in Spain, and each individual grower has a unique way of tending the trees and producing the tasty liquid gold.

Mediterranean olive trees must mature for several years before they produce olives. Careful pruning optimizes the number of olives a single tree will bear. A meticulous hand is necessary because it takes at least ten pounds of olives to produce one liter (about four cups) of olive oil.

Hundreds of olive varieties exist, but only several dozen are grown commercially around the world. Some varieties are bursting with health-promoting polyphenols, while others contain few. The type of olive used to make any particular bottle of oil is rarely listed on the label. However, for those labels that do have the information, the following table, which shows which olives are richest in beneficial polyphenols, will be helpful.

Polyphenol Content of Selected Olive Varieties		
VERY HIGH	HIGH	MEDIUM HIGH
Coratina	Bosana	Frantoio
Cornicabra	Chemlali	
Koroneiki	Manzanillo	
Moraiolo	Picholine	
Picual	Picholine marocaine	
	Verdial de huevar	

The time at which olives are harvested also plays a major role in flavor and polyphenol content. The peak time is a short period right as the olives ripen. Olives are at their prime for only about two or three weeks. Healthy compounds then rapidly diminish over the next two to five weeks.

PICKING PARTICULARS

It takes quite a bit of work to coax oil out of olives. Traditionally, trees were shaken or beaten with sticks to make the olives drop to the ground. Such tough treatment is not good for olives, however. Tumbling out of a tree and plopping onto the ground causes bruising. Soft fruits, such as peaches and plums, wouldn't take kindly to this type of treatment; they would bruise, too, and we would never think of harvesting them this way. Olives are also soft fruits that should

WHAT COLORS SAY

Olive oils made from unripe, green olives have a light- to deep-green color. Oils made from ripe olives tend to be a golden- or light-yellow color. The color of olive oil is not an indicator of quality in relationship to culinary uses; however, if you're looking to get the most polyphenols from your olive oil, choose one with golden or yellow tints because they come from ripe olives and may contain more healing compounds.

be treated delicately because once they bruise, the beneficial oils within start to degrade.

Some olive oil labels declare that their bottles' contents are made from handpicked olives. This typically denotes a better-quality oil. Some growers separate their olives into "ground" olives (those collected from the ground) and "tree" olives (those picked from the tree) and use them for different grades of oil. Many large-scale growers use a tree-shaking device and set up nets beneath the trees that catch the olives before they hit the ground.

Growers must be careful when transporting olives from the trees to the processing plant. Olives are best carried in shallow containers so they don't pile up too deeply and crush one another. Any damage to the olives can trigger oxidation and fermentation, which create an "off" flavor. Olives should be processed soon after harvest because storing them also diminishes their quality.

PRESS TIME

After olives are picked, any leaves, twigs, and stems are removed, and the olives are washed. Then it's time for pressing. Back in the old days, processors used stone or granite wheels to crush the olives. Today, stainless steel rollers crush the olives and pits and grind them into paste. The paste then undergoes malaxation, a process in which water is slowly stirred into the paste. Malaxation allows the tiny oil molecules to clump together and concentrate.

The mixture is stirred for 20 to 40 minutes. Longer mixing times increase oil production and give the oil a chance to pick up additional flavors from the olive paste. However, the mixing also exposes the oil to air, producing free radicals that poorly affect its quality.

Modern systems use closed mixing chambers filled with a harmless gas to prevent oxidation. This method increases yield and flavor and preserves quality. The mixture may be heated to about 82 degrees Fahrenheit, which further increases yield but does allow some oxidation. This temperature is low enough to be considered "cold pressed."

PRIZED FRUIT

Olives and olive oil were so valued in ancient Greece that they were given as awards to Olympic athletes. A wreath of olive leaves was placed on the heads of winning athletes, and their prize might be an amphora (a two-handled jug with a narrow neck) filled with olive oil.

Next, the paste is put on mats and further pressed or sent through a centrifuge (a compartment that is rotated on a central axis at extreme speed to separate materials). When the centrifuge spins, the olive paste remnants are pushed to the sides of the compartment cylinder while water and oil are extracted from the center of the centrifuge. The oil and water are later separated.

LABEL LINGO

Here are some terms you might see on olive oil labels that describe extraction methods. The first two are cold-extraction processes. Olive oils processed by these methods retain the vitamins, health-boosting phytochemicals, color, flavor, and aroma of the olives. The second two are heat-extraction processes. The heat used in these techniques takes a toll on olive oil. Excessive heat destroys many of the fragile nutrients and phytochemicals and just about all of the color, flavor, and aroma.

Cold pressed. This method removes the oil from olives through pressing and grinding. For the oil to be labeled "cold pressed," the heat generated by friction from the grinding must not exceed 86 degrees Fahrenheit. (Other oils, such as safflower and canola, are sometimes cold pressed, but for those oils, friction temperatures of up to 120 degrees Fahrenheit are allowed.)

Vacuum extraction. This is a cold-extraction method done in the absence of air and light at temperatures as low as 70 degrees Fahrenheit. Olives are crushed and ground, then mixed with water and churned in a device that uses a vacuum. The process ensures no air is introduced into the system and preserves the antioxidants and nutrients.

Expeller pressed. This method also uses grinding and pressing, but with extreme amounts of pressure, sometimes up to 15 tons per square inch. This intense amount of pressure creates a lot of heat and friction that takes the oil to temperatures of up to 300 degrees Fahrenheit.

Solvent extraction. This technique uses chemicals, such as hexane, to remove oil from olives. The oil is then boiled to get rid of the chemicals. The oil may then undergo additional heat processing, bleaching, or deodorizing, which leads to a bland oil, but one with a high smoke point and long shelf life.

The solid material that remains after the extraction of the oil is called pomace, and it contains residual oil. Some manufacturers will use steam, hexane, or other solvents to squeeze more oil out of the pomace. This low-quality oil must be labeled as pomace oil.

Oil may then be refined, bleached, and/or deodorized. Refining reduces acidity and any bitter taste. Bleaching removes chlorophyll and carotenoids (naturally occurring pigments that give plants their colors) and possibly pesticides, resulting in a light-colored oil with fewer nutrients. Deodorizing removes the fragrant aroma of the olive oil.

In the manufacturing plant, oil is stored in stainless steel containers at about 65 degrees Fahrenheit to prevent breakdown before it is bottled and shipped.

OLIVE OIL OPTIONS

Rich, beautiful, and fragrant, olive oil is much like wine—taste is a matter of personal preference. The many variables that go into the production of olive oil yield dramatic differences in color, aroma, and flavor. The following factors impact the taste of olive oil:

- Variety of olive used
- Location and soil conditions where the olives were grown
- Environmental factors and weather during the growing season
- Olive ripeness
- Timing of the harvest
- Harvesting method
- Length of time between the harvest and pressing
- Pressing technique
- Packaging and storage methods

Olive oils are graded by production method, acidity content, and flavor. The International Olive Oil Council (IOOC) sets quality standards that most olive-oil-producing countries use, but the United States does not legally recognize these benchmarks. Instead, the U.S. Department of Agriculture uses a different system that was set up before the IOOC existed. However, American olive growers and oil importers are encouraging the USDA to adopt standards similar to those of the IOOC.

WHERE IN THE WORLD?

When buying olive oil, you'll see varieties from all over the globe. Most of the world's supply is produced from olives grown in Spain, Italy, and Greece, but other areas, including France and California, are in on the fun, too. Here's what you need to know about olive oil and geography:

- Spanish olive oil is typically golden yellow with a fruity, nutty flavor. Spain produces about 45 percent of the world's olive supply.

- Italian olive oil is often dark green and has an herbal aroma and a grassy flavor. Italy grows about 20 percent of the world's olives.

- Greek olive oil packs a strong flavor and aroma and tends to be green. Greece produces about 13 percent of the world's olive supply.

- French olive oil is typically pale in color and has a milder flavor than other varieties.

- Californian olive oil is light in color and flavor, with a bit of a fruity taste.

Olives from different countries are often blended together to produce an oil variety. Or, olives from diverse areas of one country may be combined. These bulk-blended oils are the most economical but are still high quality. On the other hand, some producers only use olives that are grown in a specific area of a country. These regional oils are usually known for their unique flavors.

Estate olive oils are the cream of the crop. They are produced using olives from a single olive farm. These olives are usually handpicked, then pressed and bottled right at the estate. Expect to get the best flavor out of these varieties, but also expect to pay more.

MAKING THE GRADES

There are three basic grades of edible olive oil, and several types within each grade. Extra virgin includes "premium extra virgin" and "extra virgin"; virgin comprises "fine virgin," "virgin," and "semifine virgin"; and olive oil includes what used to be called "pure olive oil" and "refined oil."

All types of extra-virgin and virgin oils are made from the first pressing of the olives, which removes about 90 percent of the olives' juice. Chemicals and high heat are not allowed in the production of extra-virgin or virgin oils—no further processing or refining occurs after the pressing process. Neither extra-virgin nor virgin oils are allowed to contain any refined olive oil.

Virgin olive oils. At the head of the olive oil pack sit the extra-virgins, followed closely by the virgins. The difference between two oils and where they rank in the following hierarchy may be just half a percentage point of acidity. However, that is all it takes to distinguish between a very good oil and a great oil.

"Premium extra-virgin olive oil" is nature's finest, thanks to its extremely low acidity (possibly as low as 0.225 percent). It is best suited for using uncooked in dishes where you can appreciate its exquisite aroma and flavor. Try it in salads, as a dip for bread, or as a condiment.

"Extra-virgin olive oil" has a fruity taste and may be pale yellow to bright green in color. In general, the deeper the color, the more flavor it yields. IOOC regulations say extra-virgin olive oil must have a superior flavor and contain no more than 0.8 percent acidity, but other regulators set the acidity cutoff at 1 percent. As with the premium version, it is best to use extra-virgin olive oil uncooked in order to appreciate its flavor.

"Fine virgin olive oil" must have a "good" taste (as judged by IOOC standards) and an acidity level of no more than 1.5 percent. Fine virgin olive oil is less expensive than extra-virgin oil but is close in quality and is good uncooked.

"Virgin olive oil" must have a "good" taste, and its acidity must be 2 percent or less. Like other virgin oils, it cannot

ORGANIC OLIVE OIL

All plants have natural enemies, and olive trees are no different. Olives are susceptible to a pest known as the olive fly, which invades the olive and makes a feast of the fruit. Fungus is another adversary of olives, although olive flies are a bigger threat. Growers use pesticides, fungicides, and herbicides to protect their crops when necessary. If you'd like to avoid these chemicals, buy organic olive oil.

In the United States there are strict guidelines governing the use of the term "organic" on labels. If the label says "USDA Certified Organic," the producer has proven to the U.S. Department of Agriculture that the oil is made with olives that were grown without chemicals, among other requirements. The regulations apply whether the olives are grown and bottled in the United States or imported from other countries.

contain any refined oil. Virgin olive oil is good for cooking, but it also has enough flavor to be enjoyed uncooked.

"Semifine virgin olive oil" must have an acidity no higher than 3.3 percent. It is good for cooking but doesn't have enough flavor to be enjoyed uncooked.

Lower-quality oils. Some olive oil is further refined after the first pressing. These three types of oils can no longer bear the title "virgin."

When virgin oils are not fit for human consumption (because of poor flavor, an acidity level greater than 3.3 percent, or an unpleasant aroma), they are sent to a processing

NATURE'S PERFECT COMBINATION

Although the amount and type of oil in olives depends on their variety and growing conditions, in general, the olive offers a perfect ratio of the healthy fats.

◆ Oleic acid is a monounsaturated fat and is the predominant type of oil in olive oil. Oleic acid accounts for 55 percent to 85 percent of an olive oil's content.

◆ Linoleic acid is an omega-6 polyunsaturated fat. It makes up about 9 percent to 10 percent of a typical olive oil.

◆ Linolenic acid is a heart-healthy omega-3 polyunsaturated fat. The average olive oil is about 1 percent linolenic acid.

◆ Saturated fat and other substances, such as vitamins, phytochemicals, moisture, and other trace compounds comprise the rest of the oil in an olive.

As discussed in the previous chapter, you can see that olives offer the government's recommended omega-6-to-omega-3 ratio of 10-to-1.

plant where they become "refined olive oils." There they undergo processing with agents that might include heat, chemicals, and/or filtration. These refined olive oils become clear, odorless, and flavorless and have an acidity level of 0.3 percent or less, which gives them a long shelf life (refined olive oils' only real advantage). They are typically blended with virgin oils, used in cooking, or used for foods that are labeled "packed in olive oil."

The current "olive oil" category used to be called "pure olive oil." Today, oils in this classification are a blend of refined olive oil and a virgin olive oil. The virgin oil lends a little aroma and flavor to the final product, which can have an acidity level of no more than 1.5 percent. In most cases, oils in this category contain about 85 percent refined oil and 15 percent virgin or extra-virgin oil. Oils of the "olive oil" grade withstand heat well.

"Olive pomace oil" is made from the olive paste that is left in the centrifuge after the olives are pressed and the oil-water mixture is extracted. Olive pomace oil can be treated with heat and chemicals to extract additional oil (about 10 percent of the original amount of oil in the olives). Its acidity cannot exceed 1.5 percent. Virgin oil may be added to pomace oil for color and flavor. Olive pomace oil is edible, but it may not carry the name "olive oil." This oil is most often used commercially and is rarely seen on the grocer's shelf.

Other oils. Sometimes, cooks don't need the full flavor of olive oil, or they need a little extra taste added. Oil producers have responded to these needs by creating lite olive oil and flavored oils.

"Lite olive oil" is also called "light" or "mild" oil. These oils have undergone an extremely fine filtration process (without the use of heat or chemicals) to remove most of the natural color, aroma, and flavor. This makes them suitable for cooking or baking in recipes in which a fruity olive flavor isn't needed. The terms "lite," "light," and "mild" can be used along with "extra-virgin olive oil," "virgin olive oil," and "olive oil."

In this case, "lite" or "light" do not refer to fat content. These oils contain the same amount of fat and calories as any other olive oil (about 13 grams of fat and 120 calories per tablespoon). The classifications instead refer to the oil's lighter color and flavor.

Do you want oil with more flavor rather than less? Some manufacturers make high-quality flavored olive oils by adding sweet or savory ingredients, such as spices, herbs, vegetables, or citrus peel, to extra-virgin oils during the pressing process. Lower-quality flavored oils have these ingredients added after pressing.

Commercially prepared flavored oils are usually safe to keep and use for a long period of time, but homemade ones are not. If you create your own homemade flavored oils, make only small amounts that you can use within several days, and always store them in the refrigerator to prevent the growth of potentially harmful bacteria. The oil itself does not support bacterial growth, but the moisture and nutrients in fresh herbs, garlic, dried tomatoes, or citrus peels do.

COLOR CONSIDERATIONS

Green olive oils come from unripe olives and impart a slightly bitter, pungent flavor. Emerald-tinged oils have fruity, grassy, and peppery flavors that dominate the foods in which you use them. These oils are great with neutral-flavored foods that allow their bold flavors to shine. You can pair green olive oils with strongly flavored foods as long as they complement the oils' pungent tastes.

Olive oils that glimmer with a golden color are made from ripe olives. Olives turn from green to bluish-purple to black as they ripen. Oils made from ripe olives have a milder, smoother, somewhat buttery taste without bitterness. These oils are perfect for foods with subtle flavors because the gentle taste of a ripe olive oil won't overshadow mildly flavored foods.

STORAGE

Because of olive oil's high monounsaturated fat content, it can be stored longer than most other oils—as long as it is stored properly. Oils are fragile and need to be treated gently to preserve their healthful properties and to keep them from becoming a health hazard full of nasty free radicals.

When choosing your storage location, remember that heat, air, and light are the enemies of oil. These elements help create free radicals, which eventually lead to excessive oxidation and rancidity in the oil that will leave a bad taste in your mouth. Even worse, oxidation and free radicals contribute to heart disease and cancer.

Rancidity can set in long before you can taste it or smell it. Rotten oils harm cells and use up precious antioxidants. Even though rancid oil doesn't pose a health risk, the less you consume, the better.

The best storage containers for olive oil are made of either tinted glass (to keep out light) or a nonreactive metal, such as stainless steel. Avoid metal containers made of iron or copper because the chemical reactions between the olive oil and those metals create toxic compounds. Avoid most plastic, too; oil can absorb noxious substances such as polyvinyl chlorides (PVCs) out of the plastic. Containers also need a tight cap or lid to keep out unwanted air.

KEEP IT COOL

Temperature is also important in preventing degradation of olive oil. Experts recommend storing the oil at 57 degrees Fahrenheit, the temperature of a wine cellar. Aren't lucky enough to have a wine cellar? A room temperature of about 70 degrees Fahrenheit will be fine. If your kitchen is routinely warmer than that, you can refrigerate the oil.

FREEZING OLIVE OIL

If you need to store your oil for a long period of time, stick it in the freezer. Believe it or not, olive oil freezes well, retaining its health properties and flavor. However, its complex mixture of oils and waxes prevent it from freezing at exactly 32 degrees Fahrenheit. Folk wisdom says you can tell the quality of an olive oil from the temperature at which it freezes, but this is not true.

In fact, refrigeration is best for long-term storage of all olive oils except premium extra-virgin ones. Consider keeping small amounts of olive oil in a sealed container at room temperature. This way, your olive oil is instantly ready to use. Keep the rest in the refrigerator, but remember that refrigerated olive oil will solidify and turn cloudy, making it difficult to use. Returning it to room temperature restores its fluidity and color.

Another option is to store olive oil in a wide-mouth glass jar in the refrigerator. Even though it solidifies, you can easily spoon out any amount you need. A clear jar is fine because it's dark inside the refrigerator most of the time.

If you don't want to refrigerate your olive oil, keep it in a dark, cool cupboard away from the stove or other heat-producing appliances. Olive oil connoisseurs recommend storing premium extra-virgin olive oils at room temperature. If refrigerated, condensation could develop and adversely affect their flavor. Refrigeration does not affect the quality or flavor of other olive oils.

Olive oil will keep well if stored in a sealed container in a cool, dark cupboard for about one year. If unopened, the oil may keep for as long as two years.

OLDER ISN'T BETTER

Unlike wine, oil does not improve with age. As olive oil gets older, it gradually breaks down, more free oleic acid is formed, the acidity level rises, and flavor weakens. Extra-virgin oils keep better because they have a low acidity level to start with, but you should use lower-quality oils within months because they start out with higher acidity levels. As oil sits on your shelf, its acidity level rises daily, and soon it is not palatable.

You'll get the best quality and flavor from your olive oil if you use it within a year of pressing. Olive oil remains at its peak for about two or three months after pressing, but unfortunately, few labels carry bottling dates or "use by" dates, let alone pressing dates.

More is at issue than flavor: Research shows the nutrients in olive oil degrade over time. In a study that appeared in the May 2004 issue of the *Journal of Agriculture and Food Chemistry*, Spanish researchers tested virgin olive oil that had been stored for 12 months under perfect conditions. What they found was quite surprising: After 12 months, many of the oil's prime healing substances had practically vanished. All the vitamin E was gone, as much as 30 percent

MORE THAN BAD TASTE

Rancid oils may not please the palate, but they're really bad news for your body. They damage cell membranes; may decrease immune function; and are linked to heart disease, cancer, and other degenerative diseases. What's more, rancidity diminishes nutrient quality.

Heat, air, and light cause oxidation in olive oil, but so do the oil's aging process and enzymes that are naturally present. Many of the nutrients in olive oils are antioxidants, such as vitamin E, but as the oil ages or experiences other oxidative stress, these antioxidants break down. The oil deteriorates very rapidly when most of the antioxidants are gone. If bottles of oil in your kitchen have been sitting in the light at room temperature for more than a couple of months, discard them.

of the chlorophyll had deteriorated, and 40 percent of the beta-carotene had disintegrated. Phenol levels had dropped dramatically, too.

OLIVE OIL IN THE KITCHEN

Olive oil helps carry the flavor of foods and spices, provides a pleasing feel in the mouth, and satisfies the appetite. Liberal use of it will enhance both savory and sweet dishes without guilt because of its wonderful health-boosting properties (although if you're trying to lose weight, you may not want to overdo it, because like all fats, it provides nine calories per gram). Virgin and extra-virgin oils are best used uncooked or cooked at low to medium temperatures. Refined and olive-oil-grade oils are the choices for high-heat uses, such as frying.

An oil's smoke point is the temperature at which it smokes when heated. Any oil is ruined at its smoke point and is no longer good for you. If you heat an oil to its smoke point, carefully discard it and start over. Olive oil has a higher smoke point than most other oils (about 400 degrees Fahrenheit). Refined olive oils have a slightly higher smoke point (about 410 degrees Fahrenheit).

BRIGHT LIGHTS, BIG PROBLEMS

Light destroys oils, and unfortunately, many olive oils are sold in clear glass containers. Most grocery stores have bright lights that beat down on shelves throughout the day, and oils sold in stores that are open 24 hours never get a reprieve from the light. In a busy store, oils sell quickly and are not subjected to all that light for very long, but that might not be the case in stores that don't get much traffic or don't rotate their stock very often.

Avoid choosing bottles covered in dust (that's a sure sign they've been on the shelf for quite a while). Bottles on the top shelf or in the front of a display are also subjected to more of the damaging rays. When shopping, grab a bottle from the back of the display, where direct light doesn't reach. Some olive oil producers use green or brown bottles to keep out the light; these are the wisest choice.

TIPS FOR COOKING WITH OLIVE OIL

Although extra-virgin and virgin olive oils stand up to heat remarkably well, they do lose flavor as they're heated, so they are best for uncooked dishes. Use them to harmonize the spices in a dish, to enhance and build flavors, and to add body and depth. Olive oil also balances the acidity in high-acid foods, such as tomatoes, vinegar, wine, and lemon juice. In general, treat your olive oils as you do your wines, carefully pairing their tastes with the flavors of the other ingredients in the dishes you are creating.

Here are some ways to use olive oil:

◆ Drizzle it over salad or mix it into salad dressing.

◆ Use in marinades or sauces for meat, fish, poultry, and vegetables. Oil penetrates nicely into the first few layers of the food being marinated.

◆ Add at the end of cooking for a burst of flavor.

◆ Drizzle over cooked pasta or vegetables.

◆ Use instead of butter or margarine as a healthy dip for bread. Pour a little olive oil into a small side dish and add a few splashes of balsamic vinegar, which will pool in the middle and look very attractive.

◆ For an easy appetizer, toast baguette slices under the broiler, rub them lightly with a cut clove of garlic, and add a little drizzle of olive oil.

◆ Replace butter with olive oil in mashed potatoes or on baked potatoes. For the ultimate mashed potatoes, whip together cooked potatoes, roasted garlic, and olive oil; season to taste.

◆ Make a tasty, heart-healthy dip by mixing cooked white beans, garlic, and olive oil in a food processor; season to taste with your favorite herbs.

Turning Up the Heat?

Whether you're sautéing, stir-frying, panfrying, or deep-frying, use olive oil and this advice to make your high-heat cooking great:

♦ Always heat the skillet or pan on medium-high heat before adding oil.

♦ When the skillet is hot, add olive oil and let it heat up to just below the smoke point before adding your food. This should take 30 to 90 seconds, depending on the heat of the burner and quality of the pan. When you place food in the pan, it should sizzle; if not, the pan and oil are not hot enough.

♦ Always pat food dry before putting it into hot oil; otherwise, a layer of steam will form between the food and the oil, making it difficult to get a good, seared, crispy exterior.

♦ When grilling or broiling, brush meats or vegetables with olive oil to enhance flavor, seal in juices, and make the outer surface crispy.

♦ Use the lower-quality olive-oil-grade stuff for panfrying, stir-frying, and deep-frying. Although it doesn't have much flavor, it does hold its heat well.

THE MOST VERSATILE VERSION

You can use multipurpose fine virgin olive oil in almost any recipe. It is moderately priced despite being close in flavor to more expensive extra-virgin olive oils. Plus, you can use it in high-heat applications. Fine virgin olive oil is also the right choice when you want quality flavor but not that strong olive taste. Try these tips for fine virgin olive oil in your kitchen:

- Brush it on meats before grilling or broiling to seal in the meat flavor and juices and create a crispy exterior.
- Add to eggs.
- Drizzle over toast.
- Sprinkle on brown rice.
- Before refrigerating homemade pesto, add a thin layer of fine virgin olive oil on top of the sauce after putting it in a jar so the pesto will keep its green color.

BAKING WITH OLIVE OIL

Most people don't think of using olive oil when baking, but it's actually a great way to get more monounsaturated fat and polyphenolic compounds in your diet. Choose the lite, light, or mild type of olive oil for baking, especially savory breads and sweets such as cakes, cookies, and other desserts. Because of the filtration these types of oils have undergone, they withstand high-heat cooking methods.

Substituting olive oil for butter dramatically reduces the amount of fat—especially saturated fat—in your baked goods. And of course, olive oil does not contain any of butter's cholesterol. You'll also use less fat—you can substitute three tablespoons of olive oil for a quarter-cup of butter. (Check your cookbook for substituting advice.) The product still turns out as expected, but with 25 percent less fat, fewer calories, and more heart-healthy nutrients.

HERE'S TO YOUR HEALTH

The world is fortunate that nature has provided us with a near-perfect food. For thousands of years, people have known olive oil makes for culinary delights and healthy bodies, so enjoy it without guilt!